Affiliate Marketing Strategy

L C JINO

Copyright © 2018 by L.C Jino

All rights reserved. No part of this book may be used or reproduced by any means, graphic, electronic, or mechanical, including photocopying, recording, taping, or by any information storage retrieval system, without the written permission of the publisher except in the case of brief quotations embodied in critical articles and reviews.

Table of Contents

Introduction 1

Chapter 1: What Is Affiliate Marketing 3

Chapter 2: Starting Off 6

    Preparing To Become An Affiliate Marketer 6

    Setting Up Your Affiliate Accounts. 6

Chapter 3: Choosing Your Niche 11

    What To Promote(Sell) 11

    Where To Find Affiliate Products 11

Chapter 4: Promoting Your Affiliate Product 17

    Building Traffic/Followership 17

    Building Your Marketplace And Customer Base 17

Chapter 5: Turning Affiliate Marketing Into A Passive Income 22

    Sustaining And Expanding Your Affiliate Business 22

Conclusion 28

Introduction

Have you ever read about individuals who make six-figure income online promoting affiliate products? Most of these stories are real and there are real proofs that you can also make repeated streams of income promoting different products online.

Contrary to what many people believe, making money as an affiliate marketer is not difficult, as a matter of fact, you don't have to purchase a guide or pack, when this book has explained everything you should know and do about being successful in affiliate marketing.

Affiliate marketing has numerous benefits to the product brand owners and you as the affiliate marketer. As an affiliate marketer, you will get a percentage on each product sold through your affiliate link and marketing. The product owner will benefit from the affiliate marketing program by expanding his product reach into a broader market.

Affiliate marketing is a worldwide business that you can connect into, and with a professional website, and your affiliate link, you can market as many products as you want. The brand product owner can also save time on soliciting for customers all around the world, because the affiliate marketer can promote the product through social media, and even through word of mouth.

Affiliate Marketing Strategy

One of the greatest benefits of being an affiliate marketer is that all you have to do is promote the affiliate product. Retailers like Amazon and Click bank will do the packaging, shipment, and deliver of the products to the designated customers at no cost to you.

Affiliate marketing is always performance based, the more sales generated through your affiliate link, the more you earn. For this reason, driving traffic to your affiliate website pages, are very important to become successful. This also means engaging your followers through social media and giving them a reason to buy a product you are promoting is equally important.

As an affiliate marketer, you don't have to invest a dime, aside the cost of building a professional website, domain name and hosting.

If you are looking for a way to generate passive income even while you sleep, you should think about affiliate marketing. It is the number one sustainable passive income generation opportunity online right now and real people are making six-figure income on regular basis doing little work.

This book has been written to educate, entertain and teach you on steps to take to become a successful affiliate marketer.

CHAPTER 1

What is Affiliate marketing

Simply put, Affiliate marketing is a system whereby the merchant of a product being promote pays commission to affiliates. Since affiliate marketing is performance-based, each affiliate promoting a product gets rewarded for his or her promotional efforts towards selling the affiliate product.

As an affiliate marketer, there are so many ways you can promote an affiliate product, you can display banner ads of the products on your website and if someone clicks on the banner and make purchase on the product, you will get a certain commission, already known to you.

To make your affiliate marketing efforts even more successful, you can include special coupon codes on your affiliate ads to entice customers to click ads and purchase an item through you.

The earliest traditional methods of affiliate promotion include the use of promotional codes, coupons and referring customers to loyalty sites. Modern methods of affiliate promotion have come up and now include partnering with other professionals, institutions and even educational institutions.

Affiliate Marketing Strategy

Affiliate marketing works through affiliate networks. Affiliate networks provide a single place where you can search for affiliate products to promote with information and personalized promotional links for such products. All affiliate programs are actually administered through affiliate networks and as an affiliate, you can maximize your profit by signing up on multiple affiliate networks. For instance, you can promote same or different products from different affiliate networks such as eBay, Amazon and Click bank.

Some affiliate marketing experts will suggest that you start with one affiliate network in the beginning. This is quite true especially when you are starting the program as a fresher and you don't want to create complications for yourself. Most affiliate networks rely on the use of cookies to track progress being made by a customer, for instance, they will monitor the type of products mostly searched for by customers and the merchant carts. The affiliate network with pay affiliate marketers' commissions based on a set-rules. It is quite important to know that some affiliate network rewards marketers for impressions created (when a customer views a product several times and there is a high chance, he or she will eventually purchase the product).

While some merchants or product owners make use of an external agency to manage their affiliate programs, others rely on Outsource Program Management (OPM) software.

Subsequent chapters of this book will further discuss how to join an affiliate network and begin your affiliate marketing business.

CHAPTER 2

Starting off

**PREPARING TO BECOME AN AFFILIATE MARKETER
SETTING UP YOUR AFFILIATE ACCOUNTS.**

Though, there are many affiliates making passive income even without their own websites, but as a beginner, you cannot do without having an affiliate website. You need to create something that will become a virtual empire, and the only way you can get noticed is through your website and other online strategies. Do not try and spam social media networks with your affiliate links in order to generate some dubious sales, it doesn't work in such manner.

If you build a good Facebook or Twitter page and generate constant affiliate income, then think about what will happen if Facebook or Twitter remove your page for violating its terms and conditions. For this reason, do not rely on third parties to promote your affiliate links and generate income. Your website should be your first and primary affiliate promotion tool. You need to build a website and build your followership or readership- then link your web pages to your social network pages.

You can get free blogs or websites from Blogger, Wix.com, and WordPress, just to name a few. If you use WordPress, you will get access to numerous plugins as well as premium plugins you can purchase for little fees. With a site like WordPress, you can promote your own businesses while you are also marketing your affiliate product.

HOW TO JOIN AN AFFILIATE MARKETING PROGRAM

It is very easy to join an affiliate program, all you have to do is join through the merchant's website. For instance, if you want to sell domain names via your website, simply go the website of the domain name (for instance, iPage domain name), fill out the affiliate membership form, and you will be registered immediately for the affiliate program and then get a link that you can display on your website and each time the banner is clicked . You can also go to a third-party affiliate marketing program that offers numerous affiliate accounts that prospective affiliates can join- when you sign up through a third-party affiliate network, you can promote as many products as you want. Amazon affiliate program for instance, allows you to promote as many products as you want.

GET SERIOUS

If you just want to try your hand on affiliate marketing just because you heard some people are making income steadily, that wouldn't be a good reason to start this business. Affiliate marketing is not a "get rich quick scheme", hence don't expect it to generate millions overnight. Affiliate marketing is for those who want to earn a new skill that can be turned into a successful career. You need to learn the skills, and keep in mind that it is quite easy to learn and master the act of affiliate marketing.

CONSIDER THE FUTURE, WHILE YOU ARE BUILDING THE PRESENT

Everyone wants some instant profit right at the beginning of selling a product, there is nothing wrong with that. You need to remember, however, that your customers are directly connected to you and your business, and you must ask yourself the simple question; can I connect with this person in the future?

You need to know if they are signed up to your email list, or they follow your social media pages (including Facebook, Twitter, Instagram and LinkedIn). Never make the mistake of allowing a good commission to stand in-between you and your customers, let your website remain the lifeblood of your affiliate business, hence you must endeavor to keep your followers at all cost in order to be a successful affiliate marketer.

For this reason, you definitely need a good website with good navigation speed and simple user interfaces, to proceed with this affiliate business.

HOW TO JOIN THE AMAZON AFFILIATE NETWORK PROGRAM

The Amazon affiliate network program is perhaps the largest affiliate marketing network online right now. In 2017 alone, Amazon generates over $177 billion, through direct sales and affiliate marketing, and that is a growth of over 27% when compared to the year 2016. This revenue has made Amazon the largest retailer in the world, and this has also increased greatly the revenue of Amazon affiliate marketers all around the world. To join the Amazon affiliate marketing program, please follow these simple steps;

Step #1: Log into the Amazon affiliate website, which is https://affiliate-program.amazon.com/.

Step #2: Scroll down to the bottom of the affiliate home page of Amazon, and click on "Become an affiliate" link.

Step #3: Clicking on the link on step 2 will direct you to another page with lots of information you need for the Amazon affiliate program. Once you take some minutes to read this information, simply click on "Join now", to get yourself started.

Affiliate Marketing Strategy

Step #4: From the "Join now" link, you will be directed to a new page where you need to submit your personal and website details. Make sure you have designed a website that is live on the internet before filling this form. The information you fill here will be your official Amazon affiliate profile, hence you must ensure that the information is correct.

Step #5: The last step is to verify your identity by providing your phone number, and then click on "Call me now". Amazon will place an automated phone call to your number , and a PIN number will appear on your screen- make sure you write down thee number and type it in the space provided, to complete the Amazon affiliate program setup.

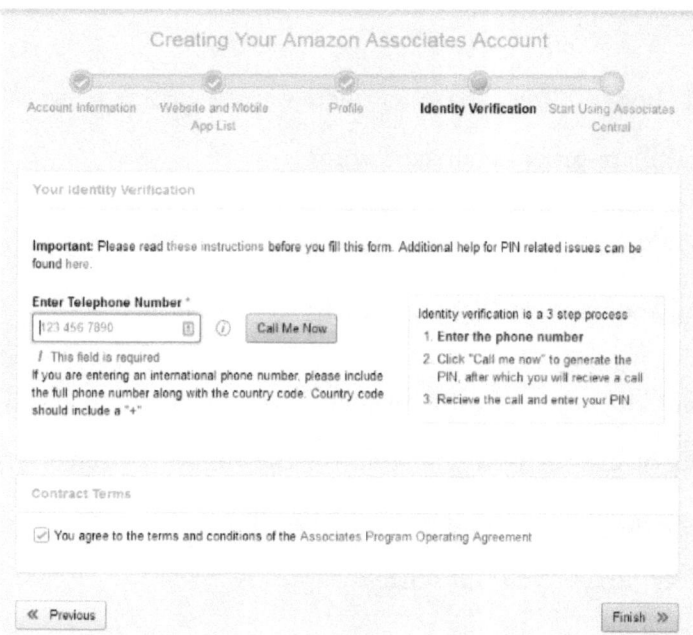

CHAPTER 3

Choosing your niche

WHAT TO PROMOTE(SELL)
WHERE TO FIND AFFILIATE PRODUCTS

Choosing a niche for your website is one of the primary steps you must take but this step can be tricky. If you choose the wrong niche, you may be promoting and selling the wrong product that may not fetch you the right amount of money you want. There are few questions you should ask yourself;

- Are people searching for this niche content?
- Is there any problem I can solve for people searching for this niche?
- Do I have adequate knowledge of this topic or is it out of my league?
- Are the competing sites unbeatable or do I have space within this niche?

It is important that you stick to a niche that you know or familiar with, one of the mistakes affiliate marketing beginners make is that they choose a topic that they are unfamiliar with because everyone else is choosing that topic. If you don't know anything about tech for instance, you should not venture into it when you know about books or educational materials. Sticking to what you do every day and enjoying doing it is very important in order to become successful, if your mind is not in affiliate marketing, you may not make a headway with it.

You need to have passion for the niche topic you write about, on daily basis, and you will be amazed at how fast you get stuck to it. For these reasons, choosing your niche topic should be brought about by some research as well as passion.

WHAT TO SELL

Now that you have a niche website, the next question should be what do I sell?

It is important to know what to sell or promote on your website because you can't just start selling anything you want. Here are some of the best available tips you should consider when searching for what to sell on the internet;

• Use the product yourself- One of the best possible ways of choosing the ideal affiliate product is to use the product yourself. Ask yourself the question; are you willing to use this product by yourself? If your answer is yes, then the product should be sellable.

• Sell a product that is directly linked to your web content- It is wrong of you to sell a product that is completely different from what your website is all about. The reason is simple, a visitor to your automobile blog will feel reluctant to buy a dog grooming product from you. If you want to promote dog grooming products, then your website should have contents relating to dog grooming.

• Consider your reputation when selling to other people. Are you sure it is a good product that will help your customers? Selling fake products on your website can harm your reputation and that means lower affiliate sales commission.

• Make sure the merchant website you direct your customer to, has a high conversion reputation. This means the rate at which web visitors are converted to buyers must be high. Consider the hard work you put in place to get such visitors to the merchant's website, hence you must be sure they are converted to buyers at the merchant's web pages.

• Does your merchant provide great after-sale customer support even after closing a deal? In order for you to convert a customer to a lead generator, you need to ensure that their requests are met, and a follow up on them is performed in order for such customers to return and buy products from the same website in the nearest future. A poor customer service support may mean a customer may never return to do business with you.

WHERE YOU CAN FIND THE IDEAL AFFILIATE PRODUCTS

Sifting through numerous sites can be boring and time consuming, however, it is a necessary step at the beginning of your affiliate business because it helps you discover the most suitable products to promote and sell. You can browse through hundreds of affiliate network where you will see hundreds of merchants that are asking for affiliate marketers to sign on them. Some of the best affiliate networks where you can find ideal affiliate products are;

- Clickbank,
- Commission Junction,
- Amazon,
- JVZoo,
- Sharesale, and
- LinkShare.

Clickbank seems to be the largest affiliate network where most people check for affiliate products, however, as a beginner you may decide to start from the smaller affiliate networks. Most of these affiliate network will pay you commission based on pay-per-sale, or pay-per-lead. Other affiliate sites such as AdSense, which is offered by Google, are Pay-per-click, which means you don't have to generate sales to earn, this could be the perfect starting point for you as a beginner. As a beginner, you can combine different products from different affiliate networks to achieve the best possible results.

Some product merchants such as elegant themes, have chosen to handle their own affiliate sales and payment through their own websites, hence, you may try and visit a merchant website when you see an affiliate product you are interested in, they do have their own affiliate links and information on how you can join their program. You need to exercise some caution when you are dealing with merchants directly, many of such merchants do not pay up commission when they are due, or they give excuses for reducing the amount of commission payable.

You may want to check your rivals' websites and see what they are selling, and then check the affiliate programs under which the products are listed. You will notice that some websites have stuck to certain products that seem not to be a very good seller, they have a reason for doing and it is often caused by the fact that there are fewer people selling such products.

You can check the AdSense banners placed on your website and then check the banner codes from Google and place them on your website also. Make sure you always follow the basic rules of placing ads on your website.

CHAPTER 4

Promoting your affiliate product

BUILDING TRAFFIC/FOLLOWERSHIP
BUILDING YOUR MARKETPLACE AND CUSTOMER BASE

Building your web traffic is very important to the success of your affiliate marketing program. It all starts with the use of the right content. Your affiliate website deserves nothing but useful content. If your visitors land on your website and they can't find useful commission, then you can forget about earning affiliate commission.

When you post useful and valuable contents on your website and you deploy the right monetization techniques, you increase your chance of getting more affiliate income. You don't have to be in a race to publish the best content, all you need to do is to publish generic content that attend to the needs of your readers, and the reason being that if someone can take his or her time to read your content, then the chances of them clicking your product link to buy the affiliate product are very high.

Make use of short and long tail keywords in your contents- these are keywords that mention the product or its usefulness in your web content. Do not make use of some ridiculous sales pitches in your content, make sure you provide an awesome information that emphasize on the usefulness of the products you are promoting, and people will eventually purchase a product found on the website. Excellent content can be described as the main ingredients in selling an affiliate product, hence do not waste the time of your readers, some good tips about generating traffic on your affiliate web pages are;

- How to use a product,
- How I used the product,
- The results I got from using a product,
- Why this product is better than the other products.

Once you have generated this content, you can close each page with an invitation to the reader to review an offer, and then they can get to see the affiliate offer on the website. You may want to write reviews, and tutorials about the product that you have actually tested. Do not think your website is not working if you are not getting the right amount of traffic at the beginning, keep doing what you are doing and eventually the results will follow.

TIPS ON GETTING MORE TRAFFIC TO YOUR WEBSITE AN AFFILIATE OFFERS

- Write guest posts on your rival's websites where you believe your potential customers might be.
- Constantly share your content on your social media pages. Do not just share once and leave, make sure you share a content as many times as you can, especially when the content is always relevant to everyday problems.
- Create a free downloadable PDF content file that should link back to the contents on your website.
- Send a newsletter or email alert to your followers' ad readers especially when you have posted a new content. This is one of the best to generate new email lists and ensure that you stay connected to your online visitors.
- Make sure you create more similar web pages and generate even more contents. There is no rule that says contents are too much on your website, as long as they keep yielding positive results.
- Make sure you check every link on your pages, to be sure that they are not broken and are always working.

USING YOUR SOCIAL MEDIA PROFILES TO PROMOTE YOUR AFFILIATE PRODUCTS

If you are not already registered on some social networks, this could be the right time to do so. Top social networks where you can market your affiliate products are; YouTube, Facebook, Twitter, LinkedIn, and Instagram. Here are some few tips and ideas for effective social media marketing of affiliate products

#1: FOCUS ON ENGAGEMENT AND NOT PROMOTION

Do not appear too promotional with your social media contents, but focus on posting on relevant contents that your affiliate product can solve. If you promote a tanning cream for instance, you should write contents about the dangers of not applying tanning creams, and at the end suggest products that provide the best tanning results and protection of skin from ultra-violet radiation.

#2: LEVERAGE ON YOUR PROMOTIONAL VIDEOS AND CONTENTS

Using the same advertisement for your social network pays best. For instance, you can share your YouTube videos about the products you promote, on your Twitter, Instagram and Facebook pages. Similarly, you can include your YouTube video links inside your Twitter and Facebook contents. This is an effective link sharing method as it gives your followers access to all your contents regardless of which social network site they are using.

#3: ENCOURAGE YOUR FOLLOWERS TO SUBSCRIBE TO YOUR CONTENTS

You need to encourage your followers on social media to get alerts or notifications when a new content is released. This will ensure that they don't miss out on any vital information.

#4: EMAIL NOTIFICATION IS OLD SCHOOL BUT STILL EFFECTIVE

Email marketing is one old but effective way to send newsletters about new deals and your web contents to your followers so that they don't get to miss out on great discounts and deals. You may include promo codes in such email newsletters. In this case, you need to ensure that visitors to your site submit their emails which you can use to build email lists.

CHAPTER 5

Turning Affiliate Marketing Into A Passive Income

SUSTAINING AND EXPANDING YOUR AFFILIATE BUSINESS

Your work as an affiliate marketer does not end with having a good website and promoting products and services from merchants, you need to perform certain tasks from time to time, these include the following;

• WATCH OUT FOR GLITCHES ON YOUR WEBSITE OR ONLINE STORE

Now that your website is just more than promotional website, you should make use of plugins from WordPress that can help you create online store. If you want an online store then you need to check the online store used by the merchants offering the product and services you promote. Make sure you check for technical glitches on those online stores, because they can cause loss of sales.

One of the quickest ways you can lose potential customers and leads is when there are consistent technical glitches on your website- visitors will definitely want to try somewhere else. You need to make use of affiliate websites that operate online store in order to ensure that referred customers can buy products directly and easily from them.

• ALWAYS REVIEW THE PRICES OF THE AFFILIATE PRODUCT YOU ARE PROMOTING

Driving traffic to your website can be very effective for you, however, you need to ensure that your hyperlinks are not broken and they are effective in directing traffic to your affiliate website. Make sure you have each product well-described with appropriate articles and keywords, and make sure their features are highlighted. In addition to this, the price on the product must be reflective of the market price. Experts suggest that affiliate marketers should aim at products within the 10-100$ price range, as higher priced items may generate higher commissions but they don't sell readily as cheaper products.

• MAKE SURE YOU ARE IN AFFILIATE MARKETING TO WIN

If you don't add new affiliate links and new contents to your website, how do you expect more readers to join your followership and generate sales for you? You don't have to write new contents every day, but be consistent with it, even if you decide to post new contents on weekly basis- make sure the content is shared on all social media pages and make sure affiliate links are included in each web page. When people want more of your contents, they simply want to visit your website as frequently as they want. If your web content does not match the affiliate product you are promoting, that could be a problem, hence you must look for the ideal product or something as close as possible to your content. Always check for the closest match to your web content.

• MAKE EACH AND EVERY ONE OF YOUR VISITORS COUNT

Do not discriminate between your visitors, the reason being that you don't know who can generate new business leads for you. You need to do your best to get their contacts, each time they respond to your content or the product being displayed for sale on your website. Try as much as possible to try as many affiliate products as you can, make sure you test them, and if they work, you can keep them on your website. Make sure you review products that are dud and remove them from your website before they harm your reputation.

When you get your visitors' contact details, you can contact them frequently especially when they have made a purchase via your site, this means you must never allow them to go empty-handed, you can give them a free web content that provides further valuable information (how to use a product, information is a good gift you can allow your visitors to download). Some potential buyers must be constantly reminded about how good a product is in order to convince them to make an actual purchase. Being persistent with such buyers will eventually give them a reason to purchase your affiliate product.

- **MAKE SURE YOU SELL TO THE RIGHT PEOPLE**

Many affiliate marketing beginners will wonder who exactly the right people are. You probably want to sell to as many people as you want, but you need to be careful about this. If your web content contains information on how to build a website for instance, the average person who doesn't know how to build a website will see it as a valuable information, whereas a computer geek may see it as an amateur content. Try as much as possible to convince novice and beginners with your contents and do not argue too much with professionals even if they post negative feedbacks on your web content- try and delete such negative contents.

Make sure that old traffic that are not generating sales are removed while the ones that are generating traffic constantly are updated with fresh contents.

- **REVIEW YOUR AFFILIATE MARKETING STRATEGIES**

Your marketing strategies at sometimes will have to be reviewed if you really want to make affiliate marketing a long-term passive income

Affiliate Marketing Strategy

opportunity. At certain points, you need to perform a complete overhaul of your affiliate marketing strategies. You need to check everything from the beginning to the end, and these include;

- Your web design,
- Your search engine optimization strategies (SEO),
- Your affiliate link placement, and
- Your social media strategies.

Your web design is as important as any other strategy on your website. Your website has to be easily navigable, which means, the total time for your website to load when visitors reach it must be very fast. Websites that load too slowly are a turn off and your visitors will definitely find somewhere else to go and that means you will lose substantial amount of affiliate income. Make sure you check the speed of access to your website from time to time and upgrade or update a web page that is not loading quickly, immediately.

Your SEO strategies really matter. Make sure you take time to generate inbound and outbound links especially from credible websites. Outbound and inbound links can be effectively used in directing even more traffic from other websites to your website. Other strategies such as keyword optimization are important because they help visitors detect your website easily.

Your affiliate link placements must be strategic. For instance, you must not overuse such links to an extent that there are too many banners covering your front page and making it difficult for your readers to enjoy your content. Affiliate banners must be sparingly used.

Make sure your social media pages are always updated, add new followers, add continue to give them information that are beneficial to them. Make sure you are consistent with your updates, and do not hesitate to reply to their concerns or feedback.

Consistency is the key to becoming a successful affiliate marketer. You don't have to spend several hours, spending at least an hour every day , on improving your affiliate marketing strategies will surely make a huge impact on your long-term success.

Conclusion

One of the greatest advantages of affiliate marketing is that it can be combined with other forms of online monetization strategies to maximize your income potential. This means you can be an affiliate marketing and at the same time you can install Google AdSense to your website to make extra income from the traffic of readers who visit your website. If you can make use of the right keyword and great linking strategy, alongside social media promotion, you can speed up the volume of traffic to your website in no time.

This book has given an insight into all necessary steps you should take in order to make huge success from your affiliate marketing program. As mentioned earlier, being persistent with the steps involved in affiliate marketing programs is the key to generating continuous streams of income. To maximize your earning potentials, make sure you conduct some research into the type of products that best suit your marketing skills. Also remember that using your affiliate product can actually give you an insight into the product's quality and that will help you write an honest review that will entice others to purchase and use the product.

www.ingramcontent.com/pod-product-compliance
Lightning Source LLC
Chambersburg PA
CBHW030552220526
45463CB00007B/3069